Blue Dog Speaks

Blue Dog Speaks

George Rodrigue

STERLING
New York

STERLING
New York

An Imprint of Sterling Publishing
387 Park Avenue South
New York, NY 10016

Blue Dog works on half title: Shades of Hollywood
opposite title page: Honesty

STERLING and the distinctive Sterling logo are registered trademarks of Sterling Publishing Co., Inc.

ISBN 978-1-4549-1342-9

Distributed in Canada by Sterling Publishing
℅ Canadian Manda Group, 165 Dufferin Street
Toronto, Ontario, Canada M6K 3H6
Distributed in the United Kingdom by GMC Distribution Services
Castle Place, 166 High Street, Lewes, East Sussex, England BN7 1XU
Distributed in Australia by Capricorn Link (Australia) Pty. Ltd.
P.O. Box 704, Windsor, NSW 2756, Australia

For information about custom editions, special sales, and premium and corporate purchases, please
contact Sterling Special Sales at 800-805-5489 or specialsales@sterlingpublishing.com.

Manufactured in China

2 4 6 8 10 9 7 5 3 1

www.sterlingpublishing.com

To Brother Edward Scanlan,
who threw me out of class for drawing

Speaking
on the
Stump

CONTENTS

INTRODUCTION

f I were to make a FAQ list, at the top would have to be, "How do you come up with the titles?" and "Do you know what you're going to paint before you start?"

Truth is I usually have *no idea* what the title or subject matter is going to be when I pick up the paintbrush. t's all about keeping things fresh. If I don't know exactly where I'm going with a painting, I have more fun; the creative process is more exciting.

These days, one thing I do know is that it will be a Blue Dog. When I began the series of Blue Dog paintings in 984, I had no idea that they would consume the greater part of my life for over two decades. The original concept of a Blue Dog was not what it is today. The idea came from a Cajun childhood story that was brought over from France by the Acadians. It simply stated that if you were not good today, the *loup-garou* would get you tonight. remember my mother relating this story many times to me as I was growing up. The legend said nothing about a dog or the color blue. But it did link this spooky werewolf creature to cemeteries and sugar cane fields and dark night skies. I thought that same sky would cast a blue-grey shade on the creature; and the red eyes of those early paintings removed any link to Tiffany, my studio dog-turned-model.

My early Blue Dog paintings were a reflection of this childhood idea and meant little beyond their connection to a ghost story. The titles, such as *Cosmos Dog*, *Missing My Master*, or *I Went to the Graveyard to Hide from the Blues*, reflected the dog's position on tombstones and under dark trees at midnight. The whole concept changed for me during an exhibition of my work in Los Angeles in the late 1980s when I overheard people call this wolfish-type *loup-garou* "Blue Dog."

Returning to my Louisiana studio, I painted Blue Dog images that reflected ideas in the present. I changed the eyes to yellow and dared to take the bayou legend out of the bayou! The titles were an important part of this transition.

Before the Blue Dog, the titles of my Cajun landscapes merely reflected a place, such as *Broussard's Barber Shop* or *Sugar Bridge Over Coulee*. They did not express a concept about contemporary life or add any extra insight to the work. But in these new paintings, I used the titles as a tool to convey further meaning. This Blue Dog could now travel in time and space away from Louisiana, away from the landscapes of the bayou, and into places where it had never gone before. I enhanced these visual ideas with titles such as *Right Place*, *Wrong Time* and *Tiffany Remembers the '70s*, and later more abstract concepts such as *All by Myself with My Happiness* and *You Would Think We Are the Same*. After twenty-five years of painting the Cajuns of the past, these new Blue Dog paintings became a vehicle for me to say things about *today*.

I feel like I'm on a journey to find an answer to each painting. Usually about halfway to completion which could take anywhere from four hours to two weeks) a title and a concept evolve. From then on. I make

the painting to reinforce that title. Yet even though the title is important to the idea of the painting, an enigma—a sense of mystery—remains, and the painting invites the viewer to fill in the blanks according to his or her own needs and experiences.

A simple Blue Dog is the obvious visual subject of every painting. However, the title combines with the paint on the canvas to convey a deeper meaning: one that in the end rarely alludes to that animal we know as "dog," but instead provides insight—whether humorous or nostalgic or sad—into the human condition. I have always said, ever since my earliest Cajun landscapes and genre works, that my work is meant to make people stop and pause, to speculate and ponder. My hope is that this process allows the viewer to become an integral part of the work's meaning. In this book you will see a broad range of subjects and titles and ideas, and I hope it helps you understand the infinite concepts possible.

Blue Dog Speaks is the first book to emphasize my titles alongside the works. In previous books, the titles were relegated to small italicized lines or indexes—or worse, not included at all. The mere fact that this book gives the titles the same prominence and space as the paintings, gives the reader a new understanding of the titles' importance.

—George Rodrigue

1

BoRN on the BaYou

Dreaming of Evangeline

I Live BY MY ROOTS

13

MY
AcaDian
HeritaGe

The

Tree

My

MaMa

Slept

Under

17

A
Voo
doo
Night

Tee

Paul's

HouSe

23

Come BAck and Lighten UP on My BluEs

Paint
Me Back
Into
YouR
Life

A

DoWn

Deep

Blue Midnight

It's Greek to Me

Again

I'm

Alone

33

Take Five

Take Five

Take Five

Take Five

Take Five

When She
Left Me
My

Blues

Got

Deeper

Valentino's
Revenge

A **Pack** of Oak Groves

A Pack of Trees

43

The Limb I Swung On

45

Rollin' on the River

A SLICE
of
Louisiana

Little Joe

I Remember This

Take

the

Picture

2

The
Other
SiDe

Resting Between the Trees

The

Re-Birth

of

TiffaNy

A Novena for Me

Missing

My

Master

63

Voodoo Will Get Me Back to You

Don't GroW Grass on Me

Don't
Step
on
my
StoNes

Dog iN a Box

The Path of the Candles

Watch Dog

3

Pure
and
Simple

It's Your Turn to Make a Move

A Palette of ThouGht

Blue

Little Blue

Las Vegas ELECTRIC LiGht Show

85

Born

with

a

GreEn

Thumb

Calling Capt. Kirk from the RED Planet

Blue

Pharoah

Looking Back at the '70s

He

Answers

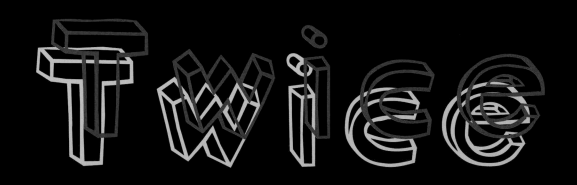

Twice

A Face iN tHe Crowd

Mickey Mouse
Has
Nothing
on
Me

(Congo Dog)

High Places

Places

for Me

101

I'M SO Cool

I'M Hot

I've

BeCome

a

Different

PerSon

Dif
fer
ent Opinions

Ancestor

Jacques in a Box

My
Line

of
Credit

On the Banks of the Mississippi

I See you Forever

She's Startin' tO Stick oN me

Rodrigue

123

FrOg

She

Called

ME a

The BLUES

Make Me feel

Like an empty Box

Box for a
Cool Cat

Reaching Out to New Friends

Me

Behind

Far

Not

Are

Memories

My

133

THE

DOG

WITHIN

135

IN YOUR FACE

Everywhere
Everywhere
Everywhere
Everywhere
Everywhere
Everywhere
Everywhere
Everywhere
Everywhere
Everywhere
Everywhere
Everywhere
Everywhere
Everywhere
Everywhere

Everywhere

Everywhere
Everywhere

4

Spiraling Out

We Are Spirits Together

Mr. Watson, Come Here .

I NEED YOU

Hurricane Romance

145

Eye of the

Hurricane

A HURRICANE of a Blue Dog

151

The Summer of '06

Crossroads of my Life

JACUZZI
WHOOZI

It

was

a

BaD

Night

I've Got to Straighten Out My Life

LOVE
Brings
Out
the
Sunshine

163

You Are My Sunshine, My Only Sunshine, You Are My Sunshine

I

LONG

for

Your Kiss

Light
My
Fire
Tonight

Circle of CANDLES

171

Candles in tHe Wind

Rodrigue

5

The
Art
of
ExpreSsion

Underneath a Warm Blanket of Love

I Am an Artist

I

DrEam

of

Being

BLUE

Night

o o

Myself

I Hear the Blues,

I See the Blues,

I Sing the Blues

183

I Can't

Get YOU

Off MY

mind

185

You're Part of my

Rainbow

HeaRts

in

LoVE

You're the Only One Under the Sun

Half

of

Me

Loves

You

I've Been Known to

Change My Position

You Got PrOBlems?

In

the

Greenhouse

Again

Red HoT SummEr of '06

A

Mardi

Gras

Night

BLACK

MAGIC

Midnight

209

Do the Town Tonight

Blue

Dog

on

the

River

213

It's Been

a

Hot Cold

Night

215

Ice

Me

Down

Wash with **HOT** Water

Play It One More Time

The Red Hot Reunion

Making Waves

225

Fall Colors for All

When the Le v e Fal l
a
e
a

s

a Leaves Leaves v

UNCLE BILL'S CHILDREN

Five of a Kind

233

You

Would

Think

We

Are

the

Same

Three

Little

Pigs

We're Not

I Look Different

Close-up

239

Totem
Dogs

241

STACKED

243

Warm Dreams for a Cool Night

245

Spring Is Coming

247

We Are Lost

Together

249

Waiting
to Be
Caught
by
LOVE

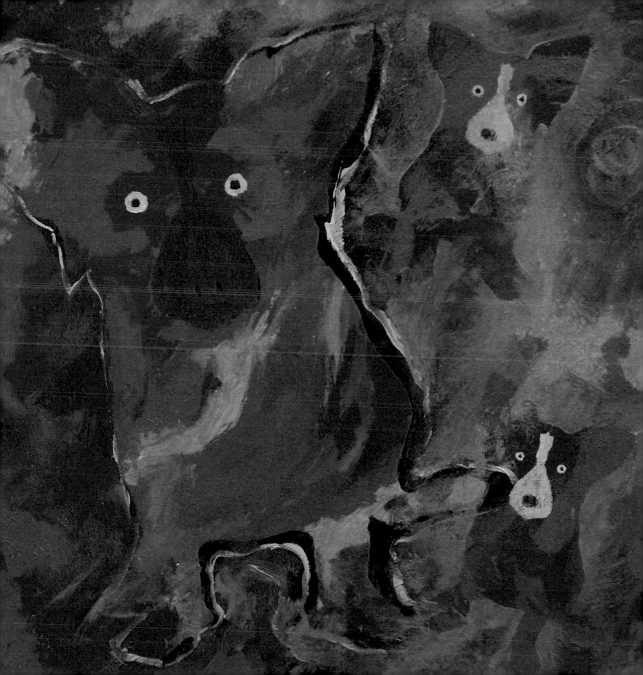

6

The Flowers of Love

Love Me, Watch Me Grow

1-800 Flowers

(I Am What I Grow)

All By Myself with My Happiness

Faith,

Hope

Charity

259

I GROW FLOWERS FOR A LIVING

I Planted

THE

Seeds of Beauty

263

From a Seed Flowers Grow

He's Just a

MEAN

Flower Machine

267

Grow

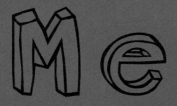

 SomEthin'

Mister

269

Sunshine Over My SHOULDER

273

Springtime in Louisiana

She's

Got

Me

Waiting

with

the

Wallflowers

She Took My Heart for a Loop When She Threw Me for a Away

I Sent My Blues Back to Her

Hawaiian

Blues

Rut

My

of

Out

Getting

285

Me

Rodrigue

287

My world is Full of Love

289

Our Love Blooms Forever

Forever Forever Forever
Forever Forever Forever
Forever Forever Forever
Forever Forever Forever
Forever Forever Forever
Forever Forever Forever
Forever Forever Forever
Forever Forever Forever

(The Day Love Bloomed)

MY LOVE TREE

Red

Hot

Kisses

Hot Poppies

297

Let's

Walk

in the

Flower
Garden

I Cannot Tell a Lie

(Don't Pee on My Cherry Tree)

In My
Heart

You'll Live Forever

Two Hearts in Love

Rodrigue

7
A
Woman
Loves the
Blues

She Drove Me Crazy

Wrong

Century

Handle My

HEART

with Care

311

Calif ornia

Dreamin'

Blue Eyes Blue Heart

Speaking to the WIND

She Brought
Color
to My Life

319

Virtual Reality

Right Place,

Another

Dangerous
Woman

Crept

into

My Life

325

She

Never

Saw

Me

Jolie Blonde

on My Mind

Here We Go Again, She's Got on Her Mind

Again

Jolie
in the
Middle

333

Multiplicity

Your Daughter's a Cowgirl

337

Peroxide Blues

341

Wendy and Me

(The Invitation)

343

The Finish Line

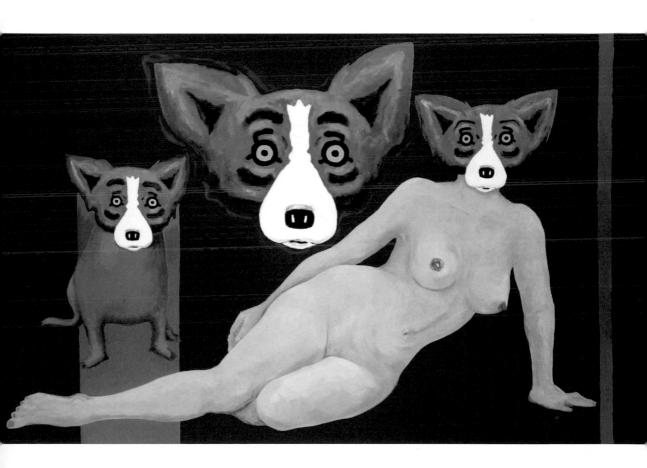

345

8

A

Dog of a

Different

Color

Lipstick on My Collar

You Never Know Who

or What

Is Coming

349

The **Blues** Can Hide

a Bad Apple

Identical Twins

Identical Twins

My

GOLD

Pet

Gold shoes

The Andrew
Sisters

359

The Everly Brothers

Three

DOG

Night

363

Sun Kiss and the Orange Peels

Gold

Blues

Me

Away

Stars

Out

Hang

Together

369

Boiling My Blues Away

371

The Birthday Party

373

Islands in the Stream

375

WHEEL OF FORTUNE WHEEL OF FORTUNE WHEEL OF FORTUNE WHEEL OF FORTUNE

Don't

Show Me

Your

Colors

379

Stoplight

381

She

Stole

My

Burning Heart

383

Angel on My Shoulder

Evermore

9
Masquerade

I Just Don't Wanna Be Me

I Grew Up a

C o w b
o

y

They All

Ask

for

BIG TOP DOG

(My Baby Made a Clown Out of Me)

395

High

I Was a King in Places

Jester

399

My

Hero,

Count

Dogula

401

Justice

Power

and

Faith

403

Phantom

Dog

405

Mardi Gras

Dog

407

Now You
See It,
Now You Don't

409

10
At Home
with the
Blues

When My Baby Left Me,
All She Left Me Was My Blue Suede Shoes

I Proved My Love
for You with
Credit Cards,

But You Were Only
Window-shopping

Hiding

from the

Blues

415

I'm Just Another Memory on Your Nightstand

A

Smarter

Breed

419

I Once
Debated
Nixon

421

TWO
SHOES

423

My
Yellow
Chair

PC
Blues

427

11

On the Road

Breaux Bridge Shoefly

431

On the Road Again

433

The Free Life

(A Faster Breed)

My Favorite Part
of Town

(I'm Just Waiting for My Turn)

437

The High Country

439

Guess Who's Coming to Dinner

441

Jackpot

443

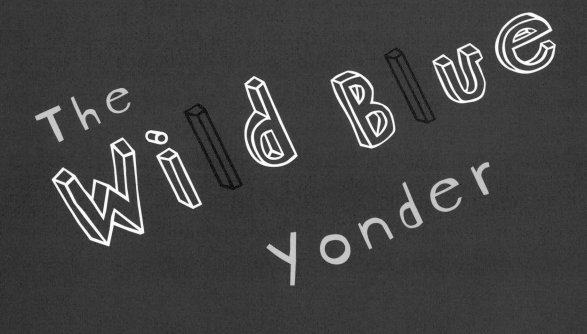

The Wild Blue Yonder

445

Life's a Blast

447

Star-
Hopping
(Export Business)

449

To Go Where No Man Has Gone Before

451

12

Taking Care of Business

My Blues Brothers

Big
Night

Tonight

455

Hot Tubbin'

You've Got My

Heart

in Knots

459

Can't
Tie Me
Down

461

Don't

Tie

Me

Down

463

I Ain't No Cartoon Dog

465

Secret

Service

Dog

467

Yuppie
Puppy

469

Wall

Street

Blues

We Make Money

the Old-

Fashioned

Way

473

13
Hurricane

You Can't Drown the Blues

We Will Rise Again

477

479

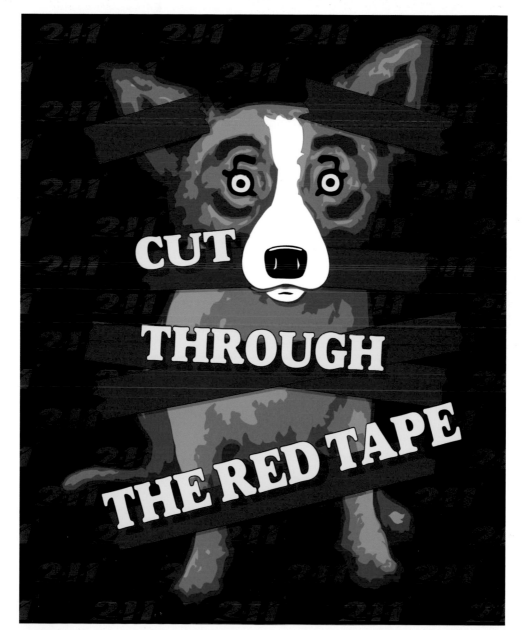

We Are Marching Again

485

14
Red, White, and Blue

Paul Revere

As Honest as the Day Is **Long**

God Bless
America

491

Star-spangled
Blue Dog

493

Star

Rising

Catch a

495

I Live for
My Country

497

My

Mood

Changes

499

The USA

503

505

Friendly Cats

INDEX